The New Camera

Angela Llanas

1 Happy birthday

Danny and Trixie live in a little house, near London. Danny is eleven. Trixie is younger than Danny. She's nine.

Mr Jackson is the children's father and he works in a bank. He goes to work at eight o'clock. Mrs Jackson is the children's mother. She's a dentist. She works in the morning. In the afternoon she works in the house.

Last Tuesday was a happy day because it was Trixie's birthday. She was nine. She got up at seven o'clock.

'Happy birthday,' said her mother.

'Is it your birthday?' asked Danny.

'Don't you know?' said Trixie.

'Of course!' said Danny. 'Happy birthday.'

'Nine today,' said Mr Jackson. 'Happy birthday, Trixie.'

'Thanks, everybody,' said Trixie.

It was eight o'clock so Mr Jackson went to work.

'Eat your breakfast,' said Mrs Jackson. 'You're going to be late for school.'

Trixie looked for her presents but there weren't any.

'Sorry, darling. We haven't bought you your present yet. We'll get it this afternoon, after school,' said Mrs Jackson.

'Can Danny come?' asked Trixie.

'Of course,' said Mrs Jackson. 'Hurry up. You'll be late for school.'

'Can I buy some sweets?' asked Danny.

'No,' said his mother. 'Sweets are bad for your teeth. I should know. I'm a dentist.'

At four o'clock Mrs Jackson was outside the school.

'We're going to the shops,' she said.

'Can we buy some sweets?' asked Danny.

'It's Trixie's birthday,' said his mother. 'We're going to buy a present for her. What would you like, Trixie?'

'I don't know,' said Trixie.

'Are we going by taxi?' asked Danny.

'No,' said his mother. 'We're going by bus. Look! Here it is. Hurry up.'

Danny, Trixie and their mother were in the shopping centre.

'I'm hungry,' said Danny.

'You're always hungry,' said his mother. 'What would you like?'

'I'd like a beefburger, please,' said Danny.

'It's your birthday, Trixie. What would you like? There's the Pizza Palace and the Burger Place. There's a sandwich bar next to the Pizza Palace. What would you like?'
'I'd like a pizza, please,' said Trixie.

2 The present

They went to the Pizza Palace where they ate pizzas. Then they ate ice-cream. Danny ordered chocolate ice-cream, and Trixie ordered strawberry.

Their mother doesn't like chocolate or strawberry ice-cream. She had vanilla. Then Danny had another chocolate ice-cream.

'Now let's go to the shops,' said Mrs Jackson.

They went into a big shop. It was the biggest shop in the shopping centre.

'Would you like a doll, Trixie?' asked Mrs Jackson.

'No, thanks,' said Trixie. 'I'm too old for dolls.'

'Would you like a football?' asked Danny. 'There's a great football!'

'No, thanks,' said Trixie. 'I don't play football.'

'I'll play with you,' said Danny.

'Would you like some paints?' asked Mrs Jackson. 'You like painting.'

'I like painting,' said Trixie, 'but I have some paints at home.'

'Well, what would you like?' asked her mother.

Then Trixie saw some cameras.
'A camera,' she said. 'I'd like a camera.'
'They're expensive,' said her mother. 'Which one would you like?'
'What about that little one?' said Trixie.
'This one is cheaper,' said the shop assistant. 'But it will take good photos.'
'Good,' said Mrs Jackson. 'You can have that one, Trixie.'

Trixie liked her birthday present. She was happy.

The next day, Trixie went to school. She had her new camera in her bag. Her teacher was in the classroom.

'Look, Miss Sandy,' she said. 'This is my new camera. My mother bought it for me. It was my birthday yesterday.'

'It's a very nice camera,' said Miss Sandy. 'You're a lucky girl. There's a school competition. You can take some photos. Look at the poster.'

3 The competition

Trixie read the poster.

'Are you going to take some photos?' asked Miss Sandy.

'Yes,' said Trixie. 'I want to take some interesting photos, some exciting photos AND some beautiful photos.'

At six o'clock, Trixie and Danny were in the kitchen. There were some dirty dishes in the sink so Trixie washed them. Danny sat at the table. He had Trixie's new camera.

'Did you see the poster, Danny?' Trixie asked.

'Yes,' said Danny.

'I'm going to take some photos,' said Trixie. 'I'm going to enter the competition.'

'The best photos will win,' said Danny. 'You can't take good photos.'

'Yes, I can,' said Trixie angrily. 'Give me my camera.'

Mr Jackson came into the kitchen. He was angry.

'Be quiet,' he said. 'You're making too much noise. I can't hear the radio. Why are you shouting?'

'Danny has my camera,' said Trixie.

'I'm going to take some photos,' said Danny. 'I'm going to enter the competition.

'I'm going to take some photos,' said Trixie.

'You can both take some photos,' said her father. 'You can both enter the competition. There's no school tomorrow. You can go out and take some photos.'

The next day, Danny and Trixie got up at eight o'clock. They went to the kitchen. Trixie made some sandwiches and Danny put some cakes, biscuits and fruit in the basket. Trixie put the sandwiches and some lemonade in the basket. Her mother put some chocolate in the basket too.

'What's the weather like?' Danny asked.

'It's cold,' said his mother. 'Take your sweaters. Do you have your camera?'

'Yes, I have,' said Trixie. 'I'm going to win the competition.'

Danny took the basket and Trixie took the camera.

They walked to the river. They saw a blue and green bird. It was a beautiful bird. It was in a tree near the river. Suddenly it dived into the river and caught a fish.

'Quick,' said Danny. 'Take a photo, Trixie.'

Trixie took a photo of the blue and green bird.

There were some big stones in the river.

'Let's cross the river,' said Danny. 'We can walk on those stones.'

'Be careful,' said Trixie. 'Don't fall in.'

'I'm not going to fall in,' said Danny. 'You should be careful because you have the camera. It will get wet.'

Danny and Trixie walked on the big stones. They didn't fall in the river and the camera didn't get wet.

4 The accident

'I'm hungry,' said Danny. 'Let's have our picnic.'

The children climbed over a gate and sat on the grass. They put the sandwiches, cake and fruit on some plates. They ate the sandwiches.

Danny and Trixie were in a field. A cow came and ate an apple.

'Quick, Danny,' said Trixie. 'Take a picture of the cow.'

Danny took a photo of the cow.

The children ate their picnic and they drank their lemonade.

'Let's go to the river again,' said Danny.

'Yes,' said Trixie. 'We can take lots of interesting photos there.'

They walked to the river where they saw a small boat. A small boy was in the boat. He stood up and waved to Danny and Trixie.

'Hello!' he shouted.

Suddenly the boy fell in the water.

'Help!' he shouted. 'I can't swim!'

The little boy went under the water. Once...twice...

'Where is he?' said Trixie. 'I can't see him.'

'There he is!' said Danny. 'He's near the big stones.'

There was a house near the river.

'Run to the house, Danny,' said Trixie. 'Ask somebody to come.'

Danny dropped the basket and ran to the house.

Trixie walked on the stones and held on to the boy's sweater. The little boy was wet and he was heavy. Trixie couldn't pull him out.

Trixie's new camera was hanging from her neck. The boy caught hold of the camera and pulled and pulled.

Suddenly Trixie fell in the river.

'Oh!' she shouted. The water was very cold.

Trixie was near the boy now so she pushed him. Slowly she pushed him towards the big stones.

'Hold on to a stone,' she said.

Danny ran to the house. A man came to the door.

'Please come!' Danny said. 'There's a boy in the river.'

Danny and the man ran to the river. The man rescued the little boy. Then he rescued Trixie.

The little boy was wet. Trixie was wet and she was cross.

'I fell in too,' she said. 'I'm cold.'

It started to rain.

'I'm wet,' said Trixie. 'Now you're going to get wet too, Danny.'

'Come on,' said the man. 'You must all go home now. You'll catch colds!'

'Where's the camera, Trixie?' Danny asked.

'I don't have it,' said Trixie. 'I lost it in the river.'

Trixie was very unhappy.

5 A nice surprise

Danny and Trixie went home.

'You're soaking wet,' said Mrs Jackson. 'What happened?'

'I fell in the river,' said Trixie.

'Where's your camera?' asked her mother.

'I lost it in the river,' said Trixie.

'But she rescued a little boy,' said Danny.

'Did you?' said Mrs Jackson. 'You're a brave girl.'

'But I don't have my camera,' said Trixie.

'It doesn't matter,' said her mother. 'You're all right and it was a cheap camera.'

'We took some photos,' said Danny.

'Now we don't have any,' said Trixie.

'We took some good photos,' said Danny.

'Yes,' said Trixie. 'I took a picture of a blue and green bird. It had a fish.'

'I took a picture of a cow,' said Danny. 'It had an apple in its mouth.'

'We took a lot of photos, but they're in the camera . . . ,' said Trixie sadly.

'Now we can't enter the competition,' said Danny sadly.

The next day, Trixie and Danny came home from school. Mrs Jackson had a parcel.

'Look, Trixie,' she said. 'The postman came. There's a parcel for you.'

'Your name is on the parcel,' said Danny. 'Come on, open it.'

Trixie opened the parcel.

'Look!' she shouted. 'What a nice surprise! It's a camera. It's a new camera.'

'A new camera?' asked Mrs Jackson.

'Another new camera?' said Danny.

Mrs Jackson looked at the camera.

'It's a very good one,' she said. 'It's an expensive camera.'

'There's a note,' said Trixie. 'It says, "You rescued me. Thank you very much. Tom." '

'You lucky girl,' said Mrs Jackson. 'You were very brave and now you have a new and better camera.'

'Now we can take some photos,' said Trixie.

'And we can enter the competition,' said Danny.

'But don't go near the river,' said Mrs Jackson.

'No fear, Mum!' said Danny and Trixie.

Questions

Chapter 1
1 Why is it a special day?
2 What do you think Trixie is going to choose for her birthday present?

Chapter 2
1 Why do you think that Danny wants Trixie to have a football?
2 What do you think the children will take photos of?

Chapter 3
1 Do you have a family photo album at home?
2 Do you have a favourite photo? Can you describe it to your classmates?
3 Do you go on picnics? Where do you go? What do you take with you?
4 Describe the bird by the river.

Chapter 4
1 What happened to the little boy?
2 Why was Trixie cross?
3 What made Trixie unhappy?

Chapter 5
1 Why were the children sad?
2 What was the nice surprise?
3 What are the children going to do?

Arab scientists

Who invented the first camera? It was an Arab scientist called El Hassan Ibn El Haytham.

El Hassan Ibn El Haytham was born in Basra, Iraq in about AD 965. He is famous for his experiments on how the human eye works.

Before Ibn El Haytham, people thought that their eyes gave out light.

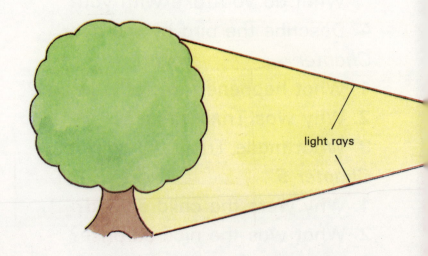

light rays

Ibn El Haytham examined the eye and did not find any light. So he did an experiment. He went into a dark room. First he saw nothing but when he lit a candle he could see. He realised that we can only see things when light comes from an object and enters our eyes.

El Hassan Ibn El Haytham's second discovery also happened in the dark room. He saw a small image on one of the walls. It was upside-down. He realised that rays of light coming through a very small hole in the door were making the image.

This discovery helped him invent the first 'camera'. We call it a pin-hole camera.

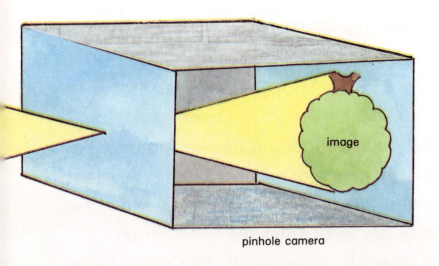

pinhole camera

El Hassan Ibn El Haytham was one of many very important Arab scientists. During the years 850 to 1500, Arab scientists made many discoveries in chemistry, medicine, mathematics and astronomy.

These scientists used books from Ancient Greece and new ideas from India. They also had many ideas of their own. Much of modern science comes from their discoveries.

One of the most famous scientists was a man called Rhazes. He made the first chemistry laboratory in the 10th century. Arab scientists invented many of the things we use in a chemistry laboratory today.

Before Rhazes, people thought that measles and smallpox were the same disease. He discovered the difference between these two diseases.

Another famous scientist was Avicenna (Ibn Seena), who lived from 980 to 1007.

Today, doctors still use vegetable drugs discovered by Arab scientists.

Do you like maths? A lot of the mathematics you do in school started with Arab mathematicians. Algebra comes from the Arabic word *al jabr* and the numbers you use in English (0,1,2,3,4,5,6,7,8,9) are called Arabic numerals.

Mohammed Ibn Musa al Khawarizmi developed them in the 9th century. Now people all over the world use them!

Do you know about any other Arab scientists?

First Things

The first lick of the lolly,
The first bite of the cake,
There is something about them
You cannot mistake.

The first day of the holidays,
The first time you wear
Something new, then that feeling
So special is there.

The first time you open
A new comic[1] the smell
Of the ink and the paper
Is exciting as well.

The very first bike ride,
The first dip in the sea,
The first time on a boat
Were all thrilling[2] to me.

The first page of a book,
The first words of a play
And the first thing at morning
When you start a new day.

John Cotton

1 *comic* a magazine full of stories told in pictures
2 *thrilling* exciting